THE TAO OF LOVE

How to Order:

Quantity discounts are available from the publisher, Prima Publishing, P.O. Box 1260BK, Rocklin, CA 95677; telephone (916) 786-0426. On your letterhead include information concerning the intended use of the books and the number of the books you wish to purchase.

THE TAO OF LOVE

IVAN HOFFMAN

Prima Publishing
P.O. Box 1260BK
Rocklin, CA 95677
(916) 786-0426

Production by Ed Lin, Bookman Productions
Copyediting by Patterson Lamb
Composition by Hi-Tech Graphics & Publishing
Interior design by Mike Yazzolino, Bookman Productions
Cover design by The Dunlavey Studio

Library of Congress Cataloging-in-Publication Data

Hoffman, Ivan.
　　The Tao of love/Ivan Hoffman.
　　　p.　　cm.
　　ISBN 1-55958-278-2 : $9.95
　　1. Love.　2. Taoism—Miscellanea.
　　　3. Interpersonal relations.
　　I. Title.
BF575.L8H637　1992
299'.51444—dc20　　　　　　　　　　　　　　　92-32925
　　　　　　　　　　　　　　　　　　　　　　　　　　　　CIP

93　94　95　96　RRD　10　9　8　7　6　5　4

Printed in the United States of America

CONTENTS

This book is dedicated to my wife, Susan, who gave me the courage to change my life; to my children, Garrett and Jordan, who, I hope, see that it is in our power to do so; to Murray, my dog, who, in giving me back more love than I could imagine ever existed, opened me up to myself; to my mother, who told me to take typing in high school — and I never thought I would ever use it; and to her and my late father, who were there at the beginning; to Rabbi Steven Reuben, who has been the spark on many occasions; to Leslie Parness, my agent, who came to me through Steve; to Susan Nero, who encouraged me to write when I never even thought of writing; and finally to Signe Taff, a most gifted astrologer who saw all of this over a dozen years ago.

I also wish to acknowledge my wife Susan's significant contributions to the chapter "How Do We Change?" Her experience as a therapist has been invaluable.

1

THE PREMISE

Life is like a parking garage: if you go backward, you get severe tire damage.

WE SEEM ALWAYS TO HAVE BEEN WITHOUT LOVE. NOT only have we lacked true interpersonal love but, as a result, we have lacked the love of the larger entity, the Earth. Perhaps the problem is that we have never really learned how to love. Perhaps the time has come for a new way of thinking about ourselves so that we can learn to love. One approach to this new way of thinking may be to seek out the wisdom of ancient thinking.

There will be no quick answers here, no magical cures, no easy solutions. At stake in learning to love is learning about ourselves. Personal growth is what love is about and personal growth is what our lives are about. The work involved in changing spans our entire lifetime, maybe several lifetimes. The approaches and suggestions I offer will not produce change tomorrow, but, followed from the soul, from the deepest part of you, they can affect who you are and how you look at yourself and, in turn, the rest of the world. That vision may lead to your becoming a more open person and to experiencing greater love in your life.

We will not find love, for ourselves or for others or for the planet, by what we have or what we have done, but rather by what we have learned from what we have or what we have done. Love is not about things but about the soul. Things are important — and I am not suggesting that they are not — but they should not be mistaken for love, which they often are.

Love is first about pain. Were it otherwise, libraries full of books about love and finding ourselves would not be necessary. This book would not be necessary. But love is about pain, and so they are and this is. Indeed, we cannot know love unless we know pain, for it is the pain itself that creates our abilities to know love.

We struggle with the pain of love because we continue to love pain. When we find ourselves "in love" we are in great pain, with feelings of probable loss, of jealousy, of anxiety, of abandonment. We have these feelings of pain because we perpetuate them out of our feelings of lack of self-worth. We are unwilling to let go of these feelings because it is better to know the certainty of the pain than the uncertainty of the new. So the feelings about the pain in ourselves simply get transferred to our love lives.

But I write not about the pain of love. That I will leave to the songwriters of the world. Rather, finding love is about letting go of pain that comes from the poor images we have of ourselves. This lack of self-worth comes, in part, from not feeling safe, from not feeling connected to the planet, from not feeling a part of the universe. The lack of self-worth comes from the images we developed of ourselves when we were children. Our perceptions of the universe formed at that early time continue to dominate our adult thinking. If we felt unsafe when we were young, we continue to feel unsafe today. If we felt unloved, we continue to feel unloved. We remain in this insecure place until our lives change and we open up to a different perspective about ourselves.

We derived this picture of ourselves from our reaction to our initial environment, from our parents. If they were still living out their childhood perceptions when we were young, what we are now dealing with is a continuation of their poor self-image, and of their parents' self-image as well. It has been going on since humanity began.

But this is not a book about blaming our parents or indeed anyone else. Just the opposite. It is about letting go of that albatross which we have for decades carried around and which has restricted our freedom and our ability to love. When we view them from the right perspective, we realize that our parents were given to us by the universe to teach us our particular lessons in life.

> Wise people seek solutions;
> The ignorant only cast blame.[1]

Our job is to break the patterns of repetition and create a new point of view for ourselves so that we can pass this healthy perspective along to our children and others whom we touch. We have an opportunity to start fresh, free of self-imposed oppression.

The struggle to love is a struggle about us. Getting free, free to love, is both the goal and the process. Part of this freedom comes simply from the struggle to become free.

THE CONNECTION

Except for our children, we join the lives of everyone else we meet *in medias res*, in the midst of things. We take them as we find them, for good or for ill. And what we find is a reflection of all that has gone before in all of our collective lives, either in actuality or in perception, which can be even more real than reality.

Each of us comes to the world of today with our own fears, defenses against those fears, anxieties, wants, needs, and so on. And in the process of interacting with others, we pass on to them some of our own selves, some of our own fears, some of our own defenses, however unconsciously. In the process of passing it along, we become part and parcel of all that is occurring in the world, even though it may not seem that way to us, even though it may seem as though we are unconnected to it all. The ill feelings we have about our own selves become embodied in the inability to give out love or to let go enough to receive it.

Because of our feelings of insecurity, we tend to

want to control the world and others in it in our attempt to feel safe. We believe that if we are in control of our world, we will be secure. It never works. But we continue to try, never wanting to admit to ourselves that it is not working, for to do so would mean that all of our perceptions about ourselves, about the universe, would be wrong. It would mean that what we have believed for eons is simply not so. It would be shattering.

The irony is that the very shattering, the intense destructiveness, bringing our house of cards down upon us, can, like the Phoenix bird of myth, be the very same power that can create our new vision. It is the tragedy that creates the opportunity. It is the feeling of pain that creates the opening.

We rarely break out of our old way of thinking about ourselves without this pain and, as a result, we get stuck, repeating relationships that have failed us in the past. ". . . [F]reedom refers to the absence of external structure. Contrary to everyday experience, the human being does not enter (and leave) a well-structured universe that has an inherent design."[2] We remain in our useless jobs, our bad marriages, our miserable lives until the pain becomes unbearable. Sometimes our tolerance for the pain is so great that it never leads to change. By not opening ourselves up to new ideas with funda-mentally different perspectives, by continually repeating old patterns no matter how destructive they are to us, we stagnate and by stagnating, we are, in truth, going backward.

LOVE IS ABOUT TRUST

Love is about trust. Love is about trust in ourselves long before it is about trust in another. Trust is about feeling secure in the universe. Trust is about feeling safe about ourselves in relation to tomorrow.

Until we can trust, we cannot love. Until we can trust in ourselves, trust that we are living in harmony with the world, we cannot love ourselves. Until we love ourselves, we can never know love with another. Trusting requires faith. Trusting means letting go of the control that we have deceived ourselves into thinking we have.

Loving another means being open and vulnerable to that other, yet knowing that no matter what happens to the relationship, we will not have lost ourselves in it so that if it ceases to exist, we will not cease to exist also. It means joining without losing. It is our fear of loss that keeps us from uniting. And it is the lack of trust in ourselves that is at the heart of the feeling of fear that leads to the lack of trust.

... [P]eace can only be made by those who are peaceful, and love can be shown only by those who love.

No work of love will flourish out of guilt, fear, or hollowness of heart, just as no valid plans for the future can be made by those who have no capacity for living now.[3]

HOW SHALL WE BEGIN?

The *Tao Te Ching,* written over 2,500 years ago but in truth many thousands of years older than that, teaches us that the world and all of existence is us.

The Tao enables us to connect with the natural processes of the universe and awakens intimate attention to our own feelings. It helps us from going into denial, onto automatic pilot, falling backward into old patterns and belief systems. The Tao is basic, elemental, simple in its philosophy. It deals with the roots, the causes, of the diseases that afflict us and, in turn, gives us a guideline for thinking about ourselves in a different way so that we can let go and be whole. The Tao tells us that we can be safe. It unites us with the soul of the universe. Taoism, with its emphasis on this unity with all things, is in truth what we are born with. It is only as we grow — some would say mature — that we lose our Taoist natures and see the world as separated from ourselves and in a dualistic fashion. Therefore, learning about Taoism is natural and takes us back to our original selves. It is far from foreign.

The Tao helps us to find love because when we

are ourselves, not defended, not afraid, we are open and whole. When we are complete, we can find love because only then will we not need another. Our relationship will be based on positive feelings about ourselves, and the weaknesses will not exist, since we will not fear loss and will not have to try to control our mate.

Taoism is about developing a demeanor and a set of thoughts that transcend the day-to-day details about which our lives are composed and being able to step outside of those details to see a larger picture. Taoism is about trying to find what God, what nature, intends for us. It helps us look and listen for the signs that, if vague, are everywhere.

By connecting us with our true natures, it teaches us that we are free and whole individuals, not victims. As a result, we are able to make choices about who we are and how we can more properly conduct ourselves so as to live full and complete lives instead of lives of misery, desperation, and untimely death.

No one is more capable of making decisions about change than each of us for ourselves. This ability creates a new way of looking at the world, for it causes us to see that ultimately it is we who are responsible for our lives. We can change our futures simply by changing our minds. We have this power.

Far from being a burden, personal responsibility

is both exhilarating and empowering. Those who have for years shifted blame for their lives onto someone, something, out there have never really touched themselves, have never really been free. The ability to feel and be anything we wish to feel and be without dependence for our definition on anything or anyone external is liberating. Victims do not make choices, for they are, by definition, subject to the whims and caprices of the other. If security is what we seek, security in love, then surely the best security can come only from the roots, from self-care. We can be secure, free from danger, free from want or anxiety, free from fear only when that security comes from within and not from without. As long as someone, something, controls and rules us, we cannot be secure, for there will always be that someone or something out there against which we will need to set up our defenses and for which we must constantly be on the alert.

Responsibility creates fear, at least in the beginning, since many of the guideposts we all learned as children and in society, and which are continually being relearned, are no longer valid. The implications of being truly free, of being responsible for our own destinies, are staggering. Freedom means creating our own structure, and this is frightening. It means that blaming the other, which we have done all our lives, will not work any longer. It means that all the crutches, all the excuses, all the reasons we have given ourselves for why we are the way we are must be trashed, all at once and forever. It means that everything we do in our lives matters. It means that there are no free passes, because we are all part of the collective world and because what exists out there is merely a reflection of who we are.

Taking responsibility is not an easy task, as tasks go, but this does not mean that because it is enormously difficult we should not, each day, do it.

In my own experience, when this freedom began to manifest itself in my life, it was accompanied by a breakdown of everything that had gone before. Old ideas, old fears, outmoded ways of thinking about myself and the world began to fall away much as crusted, dried skin falls from a healing wound. There was a gap, however, between the departure of the old and the arrival of the new, of what was eventually to take the place of the old. During that hiatus, there was uncertainty, insecurity, anxiety, fear. There was no solid bedrock on which to alight and to feel grounded.

Slowly, as I opened myself up to the process of letting go, the new became my being, at a crawling pace in the beginning, but soon in rapid and ever-increasing leaps. It was the most insecure and, at the same time, the most exciting time of my life. I wish it for you.

The responsibility for ourselves, which we discover

in the process and by the process, is the liberating part, for we see that if we have created the perceptions of the world and of ourselves that have trapped us into a loveless existence, we can also change them and open ourselves to love. We have that power.

Some would say it is naive to think in the fashion proposed by an ancient Chinese philosophy. What is naive is not trying something new, or old, to change the way we think about things. We cannot say that something will not work simply because we have never tried it. All new ideas have been the subject of laughter and scorn on their introduction.

This book is not simply about the Tao, for the Tao is not simply about a Chinese philosophy. Growth involves cross-disciplinary approaches. I have thus drawn on sources ranging from the popular to the esoteric. The truth, it turns out, is not limited to a single concept; we must be free enough in our thinking to go wherever it takes us. If this book creates more questions than it answers, it will have done its job, since it is through the questioning of ourselves that we grow. We simply do not question enough, feeling terrified to find answers that make us uncomfortable. It is up to each of us, individually, to provide the answers that work only for us.

But reading the Tao, even absorbing it, will not provide all the answers. Any attempt to explain the

Tao will, of necessity, fall short, for it is an attempt to explain the natural processes of the universe and perhaps, in another fashion, the way God thinks. A difficult task at best. And so, like all spirituality, what cannot be explained by logic, what cannot be understood with the rational mind, must, of necessity, be taken on faith. Faith, as we shall explore later, comes only to those who are willing to let go and give themselves over to a larger-than-themselves process. It requires that person to be able to see the process in his or her own life. It is a subtle way of dealing with life, one that does not come very easily to most of us. It requires us to let go of the control over the universe that we mistakenly believe we exercise.

Like all things external, the Tao will not provide you with anything that does not exist inside of you. It may give you a new language with which to think about yourself. It may give you a new perspective in which to see yourself in relationship to the universe, and that, in turn, may open you up to feeling more secure about yourself. But in the end, what you feel you lack is already inside of you and you need but to find the most appropriate way to unlock your own secrets, your own potential.

> There are those who seek the Tao beyond the four seas without finding it, and there are those who have it in their bodies without seeing it.[4]

The teachings of the Tao are not about becoming an introvert, about isolating ourselves from the world as a whole and living an ascetic life. Far from it. The teachings are ultimately about participating in society according to the natural laws of the universe so that we live in harmony with its processes and not in confrontation with them.

In the end, this book is about getting free. Getting free means breaking the incredibly strong bonds that have held us tight and fettered for eons. It means getting free of poor perspectives. It means getting free of lack of self-love. It means finding a new definition for ourselves. In the end, it means translating this new definition into one applicable to the planet as a whole.

For there is another love about which I speak. It is the love of the planet. By feeling united with it, we realize that we must love it, that it is our home. I began my process with myself and found myself soon becoming concerned with the world. I found the inner peace to understand myself first and then realized that there were larger issues that I felt compelled to address. In the process, I learned that nothing out there will change—whether it be the state of nuclear arsenals; whether it be the lack of progress in ending prejudice and bigotry of races, religions, or sexes; whether it be cleaning up the ever-growing level of toxic wastes being generated each day; whether it be in developing alternative ways of resolving our inevitable differences of ideologies short of killing—nothing will be altered unless we begin to take personal responsibility for our lives. Each of those problems is but the symptom of a lack of good feeling about ourselves, extrapolated onto the larger canvas.

Most of us do not think it is true. Most of us do not recognize fear for what it is, for to do so requires us to reach inside and give up the perennial "other." As long as we are the victim, there must be a victimizer. As long as we fail to take control over and responsibility for ourselves, we will continue to view ourselves as apart from the rest of the world and can believe that the rest of the world is doing something to us. It will continue to remain "him or me," "them or us," "either/or." It is only by coming to understand that *them* are *us* and that we can and do create our own reality that we can begin to accept responsibility. By accepting responsibility, we become free, for then no one can challenge our security.

In its simplest form, the *Tao Te Ching* is about choices. It is about the choices we are each free to make about how we will live. It empowers us to act, not as automatons, but as individuals.

And act we must, for if we perpetuate the "business as usual" attitude of not thinking, of simply repeating, not only will we not find love but we will die. The odds clearly favor death. Death can occur either by an act of conscious commission or by an unconscious act of omission. Life can occur only by overt choice. Death can result from apathy, but life must be chosen intentionally. So death has a two-to-one advantage. As a result, we are made participants in our own death if we do nothing. We have no choice but to change. If we do nothing, we are in reality going backward and run the risk of impaling ourselves on the spikes of the parking garage of life.

I write not as a therapist, for I am not a therapist. I write not as a psychologist, for I am not a psychologist. I write, rather, as one who has lived with the pain and has learned something from it. I simply want to share my experiences with you. I see in Taoism another way of looking at myself. Ultimately, all ways in the universe end in the same place if the ways are true. None of us is complete. We are all in the process of evolving, of growing. I fall backward as much as you, but what the pain has taught me is that I can switch gears, get into drive a bit more quickly each time. I do not ignore the pain, for I know that it is as important as progress.

2

A WORD (OR TWO) ABOUT PERSONAL FAITH

If everyone had faith, there would be no need for anyone to have faith. Everything requiring faith would be self-evident. It is only because most of us lack faith that having faith is so important. These seeming contradictions are what having faith is all about.

IN THE "REAL WORLD," THE ONE WE DEAL WITH EACH day, living in accord with the Tao, having faith, is difficult because we have absorbed interests and ideas that go back decades in our individual lives. When looked at universally, these ideas can be traced to the very beginnings of recorded human history, or perhaps further. What seem like natural actions to some are in fact simply a continuation of the unnatural conduct of their parents and their parents before them, and so on. By the term *parents* I do not mean any particular set of parents but rather a reference to prior generations who have been influenced by previous generations. All of us have, in addition, been influenced by societal "norms," which have resulted from the acceptance of certain ideas as being "natural." [I say these are unnatural because they are forced, coerced, and not arrived at by letting the universe take its course.] Were we to be able to let go of these processes we could find peace and love. We would see that events left to their natural unfolding might find their own level. We could find harmony.[1]

> True mastery can be gained
> by letting things go their own way.
> It can't be gained by interfering.[2]

The way to understand and in turn apply these principles is not easy. Sometimes it is that way with simple ideas. There are no logical parameters, which are important to most of us, to enable us to accept these ideas. The process of changing minds of necessity involves rational thought. "The intellectual brain can only dominate awareness by affixing itself to something definite and bounded."³ With the Tao, however, it is the very nature of the process that demands there be no such concrete guidelines. What is necessary is that we learn to let go of control, which is implied in the logical thought process. Rather than thinking we are in control and using our minds to convince ourselves of it, we must learn to give ourselves over to faith. This is part of the conscious choice we must make.

Making a deliberate choice to let go of a rational thought process seems a contradiction in terms. How can we consciously choose not to think? In truth, however, there is no contradiction, for the process of letting go that which we have always been taught to think involves the heart as much as the brain. We must learn, consciously, to suspend our need to have rational answers for everything. Rational answers will come, of their own course and in their own time, when we have opened ourselves up to alternative ways of thinking. Thinking about changing the way we have thought must involve letting go the left-brain concepts that everything must follow, in lockstep, from the prior. It means not allowing the brain to overrule our hearts. The Tao speaks to the heart. It is in our hearts that faith reposes.

Giving ourselves over to the natural way, to the Tao, would also seem to contradict the need for personal responsibility. But again, there is no contradiction. It is we, each of us individually, who must choose to believe in an ordered universe into which we fit. We have the freedom to believe, to choose, this peaceful way or a way that confronts that same order. We are not destined to follow any course. Learning to see the order in the world gives us a feeling that we are part of that order, and if we can open ourselves enough to feel it, we have a sense of being more connected and, therefore, safer. It is our free choice to feel this way or not.

At times it appears that we want to change but are simply afraid of doing so because our logical mind tells us that we have no other choice except to do it the way we have always been doing it, whatever "it" is. We try to think our way through the problems. But in fact, while we must always use our minds, for that is our virtue as humans, we must, at times, suspend the purely rational thought process and think in terms far broader than that rational thought process can take us. We have to believe that there are things we do not know. When we get to the point where we believe we are safe, when we see our connections to everything and understand that we are secure as a result, then we can begin to think rationally again and develop concrete solutions to the problems we face. But at first, we must go on faith. We need faith simply to give ourselves the power to stop doing what we have been doing. Once we believe, then we can become creative with ourselves and try new ideas.

How Can We Develop Faith?

Developing faith is an internal process. Faith cannot come from something outside of ourselves. It is learning that the key to our security, our happiness, our peace comes from within our souls. Our attempts to control the world come from thinking that this security comes from an outside source that we must control.

> ... [P]art of the problem that many people have in their pursuit of happiness [is that] [t]hey think there is something that will make them happy if they can just get hold of it. They expect happiness to happen *to* them.[4]

Faith is a tricky and illusive thing. Faith can be a belief in oneself, in the universe, in that which we call God. Faith is, by definition, undefinable. Archie Bunker once told his meathead son-in-law in *All in the Family* that "faith is believin' in somethin' no one in their right mind would believe in."[5] But it is only when we give ourselves over to faith that the universe can act through us. Until then, we block and stifle ourselves by our attempts at controlling that universe.

The faith about which I speak is a faith that everything will turn out right. We are not always given

things we want but always things we need. What we
need means what we need for our growth and
development, as individuals and, in the aggregate, as
a species. It all depends on knowing what to look for.
Think of the Tao as some sort of radar that helps us
find what to look for amid the innumerable blips with
which we are constantly being bombarded. Having faith
means that we can trust enough to let go of everything
we have tried to control about life and give ourselves
over to this belief. It means believing that trying
something new will not lead to disaster but will teach
us and perhaps open us up to new ideas, leading to
new solutions to old problems. Having faith means
that we will not be afraid of the new.

It is inherent in the nature of faith that we constantly
seek proof that our trust is reinforced. It is absurd to
expect that mere mortals can believe that God exists,
for example, merely on faith. God must continually give
us reason to believe in God's existence. It does not matter
what God did for us yesterday. It is more important
to ask: "But what have you done for me lately?" One
burning bush here and there does not suffice for the
daily stresses we all go through in our individual lives;
the sheer magnitude of the world's destructive forces
we live with each day quickly turns us back into idolaters
at the altar of conformity and control. To have faith
and trust under such pressures seems superhuman.

Where is the daily proof that there is a plan to the universe in which we can trust? What level of trust does it take to be able to let go and find true peace?— a level, to be certain, far beyond the capacities of most of us. To have faith in the face of real world terrors requires—well, it requires an act of faith.

The irony, of course, is that it is in our times of crisis that we most need to be creative with ourselves. It is in these times when everything about ourselves tells us to be safe, to be secure, that we think that control is the way to achieve safety and security. It is not so, but it is easy to understand how we have come to believe that it is. Fear takes over and trust is nowhere to be found. Fear leads to further attempts to control others in order to abate our feelings of fear. Since that never works, it leads to further attempts to control and the spiral continues.

We lack faith for many reasons. We lack faith because we do not have a sufficient sense of self-worth to enable us to let go of the need for control so that we can trust. We lack faith because most of the world seems very much out of control and it seems foolhardy to let go in the face of such chaos. We lack faith because we do not have an alternative vision of what our world can look like if we let go this tight rein we keep on ourselves and others. We have never been given anything like the perspective of a new vision. How can anyone, no matter how strong, let go of that which he or she has, however unsatisfying it is, unless there is something to replace it? Without a new vision, what we face is nothing but emptiness, an abyss, a void. Letting go of that which we control in such circumstances requires the deepest belief in ourselves and, in turn, in God.

New visions can come from parents, from teachers, from others whom we respect, and without such guidance we are lost. Surely, vision also comes from individual growth, from individual enlightenment, but that too needs someone to assist in our development. Since our teachers lacked vision, they taught us without vision and thus we lack vision.

Indeed, we all lack vision because we do not see the larger order of things. This failure comes because since our beginnings, we have chosen simply to accept what those who came before us have believed.

When we look out into the world in search of new visions, we are deeply disappointed. There is virtually no one in a position of leadership, of guidance, with any new vision. Our leaders lack vision because we never demand leaders with vision. And because we never demand leaders with vision, they never step forward. Those with any imagination at all of a new way of doing things are quickly trampled in the crush to conformity.

The vision we need to make this leap into a new way of thinking can come only from within ourselves.

Change will occur only when we, individually, elect to change who we are. Forget about changing the world. Change yourself first. When enough of us change, the world will look different.

The struggle is not with an "enemy" out there but is, in fact, within ourselves. It is a struggle to get from seeing the world as a place of conflict manifested in the outer to seeing it as essentially a reflection of our own internal processes. This is not to imply that struggle is not present. Struggle is an integral part of the process, but the real question is not whether but whither the source of that struggle.

Everything that we are, everything that we see, everything over which we contend we have no control and are victims of, is but a reflection of the world we set out for ourselves. If we look for evil, we shall surely find it. If we look for conflict, that will be present as well. If we look for danger, we shall find only danger. If we believe that the world is full of "sound and fury, signifying nothing," then that is what it will be to us.

Surely there are the "real world" events with which we must deal. But it must be apparent that the world is not the same to all people at all times. Reality is not uniform. It does not show itself equally to all. Where some see only hatred, others can find kindness. Where some see misfortune, still others are able to turn that misfortune into opportunity. Reality varies according to the viewer, and when we say that we can create our own reality, clearly most people are doing just that.

What we each do is to first decide what the world is all about and then only secondarily seek reinforcement of that decision in the real world. We decide what the world is like based on our background, our childhood, our environment as we were growing up. At each stage, we seek out "truth" to justify our conception of the world.

Not only is it important to us to be right about our worldview, but it is also important not to be wrong. "[B]eing wrong is one of the most unsettling experiences that can happen to anyone."[6] Being right is just half the battle. The fear of being wrong is even scarier since if we are wrong, it tells us that our entire worldview may be false. Everything in which we have believed may be incorrect. Now what will we do? Where are we to plant our feet?

Each day that we find evil, that we find bad things occurring, we find further reinforcement of our initial, early perceptions. And very soon the initial perceptions become true, become the real world. Because in truth, there are bad things, there is sufficient evil out there to make ourselves right about what we believe the world to be. And the more we look for these things to justify our judgment of the world, the more we find we are right. As a result, we discard everything that points to a different conclusion.

If we have not been fortunate enough to grow up in a utopia, in a truly peaceful environment (and who among us has?), then we must find a way to break the cycle of perception-breeds-reality by breaking the perception, not the reality. Reality will change when our perceptions change. It is a process of growing, learning, seeing the world from a different point of view that is what life is all about. It is an extremely difficult and subtle process. It requires great strength and patience. The Zen saying is, "A tenth of an inch of difference and heaven and earth are set apart."[7]

BACK TO THE TAO

If we want to believe that the world is a peaceful, loving place, it takes more strength than most of us possess and more skills than many of us are born with to see through the evils. To see the world in this way is what growing is about. This is where the Tao can help. This is a place to begin to see how we are connected to everything and, as a result, how everything is perfect and that there is nothing to fear by letting go of the control we have exercised over time. The Tao shows us that by cooperating with events instead of attempting to dominate them, we can reach a place of peace with ourselves, a peace based on harmony with these events. The Tao leads; it does not coerce.

The great trick of life is to learn what the process is all about. It is to understand how we get from seeing only misery and suffering to finding learning and wisdom from its lessons. It is clearly not easy and it takes a lifetime, if not several, to master. If we do not learn, we shall be forever doomed to repeat the past. We shall forever find reinforcement for our notions that only evil exists because we are unable to transcend its grasp and hold over us.

The new vision that is required cannot be developed without faith. We must learn faith that we are all one, that we are all part of the same planet. Faith is required for us to know that our fear is only about fear.

But to accept all this requires faith.

3

BALANCE, HARMONY, AND CHANGE

Everything in the world is in a state of relationship to and equilibrium with something else, sometimes to many other things. Nothing exists by itself, in a vacuum, without being connected in some way, however subtle and imperceptible to the unobservant.

I REMEMBER, FROM MY YOUTH, IN THE VERY EARLY DAYS of simple black-and-white television, rushing home from school to watch Mr. Wizard. I remember one of the experiments he did involved a large glass tank, much like a fish tank, filled with water and containing a pumping device at one end. When the motor was turned on, the pump created a series of waves within the tank as the water was pushed to one side and then released. The waves would pile up at the end of the tank, ever so briefly, and then swing to the other side. When they reached this end, they would pause for just an instant and then return to the side from which they began. As long as the machine was on, the wave motions would continue indefinitely. When the machine was turned off, the undulations continued but gradually subsided until the water reached a steady state, an equilibrium, a place of rest.

There was a subtle, almost imperceptible tension that was created as the waves reached the extreme of their movement at the end of each side of the tank. The water, compressed as it was against the side, was not in a natural state. Its natural tendency was to release and expand and be free of the force created by the pump, pressing it to the glass.

Much as the water in Mr. Wizard's tank was the subject of external forces that kept it from being at rest, our lives are similarly subjected to unnatural forces that keep us from reaching an equilibrium, a balance, a steady state. These forces exert their influences on events and people and thus coerce the natural processes that would result were the pressures of these forces to be released and the events left to find their own level of equilibrium. These forces are, for the most part, created by us. We are thus the external forces and the subjects of those forces. We are both the action and the reaction.

We can hold back neither the coming of the
    flowers
nor the downward rush of the stream;
sooner or later, everything comes to its fruition.[1]

The Tao teaches us that we must act in accordance with the natural order of the universe, the natural order being called Tao, the way. It means turning off the coercive pressures that are our attempts to control the world. Conduct that is natural, unforced, in accordance with this natural order is called *wu wei*.[2]

If we let go of our attempts at controlling the world and allow it to find its own level, it can find a level of peace and harmony. Each of us, in our individual lives and then collectively, as a planet, must act in accordance with the natural order of things for this to happen. We must strive, individually and collectively, to identify and then eliminate the forces we create for ourselves, which prevent us from following the Tao.

YIN AND YANG

When everyone knows beauty as beautiful,
    there is already ugliness;
When everyone knows good as goodness,
    there is already evil.
"To be" and "not to be" arise mutually;
Difficult and easy are mutually realized;
Long and short are mutually contrasted;
High and low are mutually posited; . . .
Before and after are in mutual sequence.[3]

The symbol that appears at the beginning of each chapter represents the Taoist principle of continuous change within sustained balance. To avoid excesses brings peace since one excess only leads to the opposite pull of forces. The key to understanding balance, harmony, and equilibrium lies in understanding the Chinese concept of *yin* and *yang*. These terms describe not opposites, not things in conflict, but merely two harmonious aspects of the same thing. In many respects, *yin* and *yang* describe the entirety of the universe, and when we understand that everything is in balance and relationship with everything else, then we grasp the notion of our inter-relatedness, together and to everyone and everything else on the planet.

Yin is often considered related to the feminine side of energy, and *yang* to the male side. There is no implication in either category that one is good and the other bad, one to be sought after and one to be shunned. The very nature of the Tao is that everything is part of everything else; everything is related and connected to everything else and there is no good and no bad.

In many ways, *yin* and *yang* are similar to the Zen Buddhist notion of non-duality. Everything is one even though it may look like two.

> We say our practice should be without gaining ideas, without any expectations, even of enlighten-ment. This does not mean, however, just to sit without any purpose. This practice free from gaining ideas is based on the Prajna Paramita Sutra. However, if you are not careful the sutra itself will give you a gaining idea. It says, "Form is emptiness and emptiness is form." But if you attach to that statement, you are liable to be involved in dualistic ideas: here is you, form, and here is emptiness, which you are trying to realize through your form. So "form is emptiness, and emptiness is form" is still dualistic. But fortunately, our teaching goes on to say, "Form is form and emptiness is emptiness." Here there is no dualism.[4]

Thus, the goal for our individual lives is to achieve a balance, a harmony, both within ourselves and in turn with nature and the natural processes that are ongoing in the world. We are to strive to achieve action that is *wu wei*, that goes with the flow, that does not fight against the forces of the universe. When we are able to find this balance, this harmony, our lives will be in balance, in harmony, and we can find love, for there will be nothing that can disturb that love since we will be in accord with the universe.

To be in balance and equilibrium is not, however, to be equated with being static and immutable. In ancient Chinese culture, change refers to change that is in harmony with the universe and in which balance and harmony are preserved. So when we fear change, when we resist it, we are really fighting the natural and harmonious processes in our lives.

If we were able to eliminate the pressure on ourselves that we create by these unnatural forces, our lives and all the situations we face would be free to move but to maintain balance with nature at the same time. Of course, it is that very changeability that creates the fear in us and it is this fear that gets translated into resistance.

As the opening indicates, everything in the world is in a state of balance with everything else. Such is the nature of the *yin* and *yang*, of the Tao itself. There cannot be winter without spring; there cannot be life without death; there cannot be happiness without sadness.

> If we know the wisdom of the beginning
> And ending,
> We will never fail.[5]

Whenever one component of that relationship changes, by definition the other component or components must also change to maintain the equilibrium. There can never be a state of disequilibrium in the natural scheme of things, for out-of-balance situations, both in nature and in the lives of human beings, will always attempt to right themselves, much like water seeking to find its own level once the pressures are turned off.

However, in human affairs, the simple reality is that when this change occurs in the first element of the relationship, we fight to resist the change and thus create a situation that is out of equilibrium. In nature, on the other hand, this all occurs symbiotically unless pressures from man prevent the changes from taking place. It is ordered, destined, almost mathematically precise. It is Darwinism, it is natural selection, it is $E=MC^2$, it is God unfettered. (It is, of course, well to remember the words of Kurt Vonnegut when he said that anyone is a fool "who thinks he sees what God is Doing. . . ."[6])

OPENING OURSELVES TO UNCERTAINTY

Attempting to fight the process of change involves struggles to make steady that which is inherently unsteady.

It is control. It is a situation created by external pressures and thus pregnant with change, but in which change is ardently resisted out of fear of the very process of change. Change is what is natural, and to fetter and restrict this process creates tensions. Over a period of time, change will, of necessity, if left alone, lead to balance. Everything in the universe changes, naturally.

The symbol of *yin* and *yang* is such that as a situation reaches one extreme it merely gives way to the beginning of another aspect of that same situation, and when that second aspect reaches its end, it simply is the commencement of yet another aspect of itself. The cycles are continuous and there are, in fact, no beginnings, no endings, just cycles.

In the real world, understanding the concept of *yin* and *yang* leads us to see that we create an unnatural restriction for ourselves when we narrow our choices down to one or the other, either this or that. The very nature of the universe is that it is filled with multiple options, and we only narrow our possibilities out of fear of the sheer volume of all of them.

Trusting the cycles, which is the same as trusting in the universe, in God, requires a very different perspective about ourselves. This trust allows us to accept differing views and alternative solutions that may seem odd or frighteningly new. This new perspective toward which we are working allows us to see ourselves as a part of the larger picture and gives us a sense that we can let go of the control because we are living in harmony and balance with our surroundings instead of trying to dominate them. Given this view, we can see how we got to where we are. Trusting that we are safe in the world allows us to think about visionary ways out of those problems we now face, free of fear. Trusting that we are safe allows us to free ourselves and by this, we open ourselves to love.

This long view tells us that, in addition to the substance of our lives, there is also the process. In addition to the things that happen to us, there is the why and how they happen. The ability to see our lives from the inside, from the subjective, the feeling, and the participating perspective, while at the same time also being an outside, objective observer, may be the most important aspect of learning what trust and ultimately peace are truly all about.

Part of what we see is the series of connections that form the plot, the story line, the screenplay, the leitmotif, the how of our existence. Our lives, no matter how disjointed or unconnected they seem to be, are in fact nothing more than an orderly "but for" sequence. But for having met this person, I would not have been doing what I am now doing. But for this event not occurring, which I thought was so important to whatever I was doing at the time, I would not have had that one happen, and so on and so on. These connections are not only the structure of who we are but also form an integral part of why we do and feel and think the things we do. They are the enabling part of ourselves, and when we develop the ability to be objective about ourselves, give us the ability to see threads that form an insight into our future as well as help us see the lessons of our past that give us a clue as to what our life is all about.

As we follow our lives in this "but for" fashion, we may see patterns emerging which, when the dots are connected, seem to form a direction and from that direction, a sense about where we may be headed seems to become apparent. It is not always clear and not always true but, if we know what to look for, how to distinguish the things that happen from the reasons they happen, perhaps it is God speaking, the Tao making itself apparent. We can see a sort of cosmic "Walk This Way" sign, giving us the ability to trust in the universe and act according to its seeming processes instead of trying to control it.

Let me give you an example. It is my "life story" from this point of view. When I was very young, my father and mother divorced and my father moved to California. That event devastated me for decades and formed the crux of most of my poor self-image for much of my early adult life. But I traced my life patterns in this "but for" manner and found out some interesting things.

But for my parents' divorce, I would not have made many early trips to Los Angeles during my teen years and would not have come to UCLA. And but for having made that decision, I would not have gone to law school, for it was the strong presence of my father that, I felt, pressured me into that decision. And but for having gone to law school, I would not having gotten a particular job and would not have met one lawyer who was in the music business, and would not have gone to work for him. And but for having gone to work for him, I would not have represented one client who asked me to go to a meeting where some newly formed anti-nuclear organization was going to discuss doing something with her songs. From that meeting, I grew interested in that issue. And but for having become interested in that issue, I would not have been asked to speak and then teach at a university in Venice, California, and if that had not happened, I would never have met my present wife and would never have known the growing sense of love that I could never have even assumed ever really existed.

And so what I learned is that the "disaster" that formed my early childhood was in fact not a disaster at all but an enabling event to set the rest of my life into a pattern that has brought me joy and peace. Like the *yin* and *yang* itself, joy and love grew out of pain and no love.

This feeling of connectedness, of synchronicity, of events is what I speak of as "the process" of our lives.

It is in this process that God, that the Tao, speaks to us and tells us what our lives are about. We cannot understand this perspective unless we take this long view, a view from the outside that tells us there was a before and there will be an after. And the before helps us explain the now, which in turn gives us a clue to the after.

By seeing these connections, we get a sense that not only does the universe have an order, but that we fit into that order. We have a place in the vastness of things and finding that place can provide us with a feeling of peace. It can take away our fears, for now we know that we are being guided. We must, to be certain, have the ability to see these signs, and that is where letting go and looking for them comes in. While we can never be certain of the future, we can at least see that we are on a path and that if we stay on it, we can be safe.

This notion of spirituality gives us a feeling that the work we are doing has a context. It enables us to make order out of disorder. It enables us to open up to ourselves and then in turn to others and to accept newness and change. No doubt it takes great strength and a long view to be able to deal with and see beyond the immediate defeats the world hands us. But it is a belief in the presence of something significantly larger than ourselves that gives us that strength and that view. All that I have been writing about, about trust, about self-assurance, about independence, are in fact different words for the same idea.

Are these really signs from God? Is this really tapping into the universe? Who knows? But if it works for you, then that is the truth. Learning to read these signs and giving ourselves over to their apparent significance is what the Tao can teach. These signs are the natural order, the *li*, the *wu wei* of our lives, and trying to fight them, trying to live our lives in contravention of them, leads only to frustration and anger.

It is worth noting that there is no need to get bogged down in the free will versus determinism issue. It is like arguing how many angels can fit onto the head of a pin. Taoist thinking is such that we must be open to many variations of possibilities, not just either this or that. We are free people, given unlimited choices, some of which involve believing that there is a plan to the universe into which we can fit. Since there is no proof of any theory, if believing in this idea gives us peace of mind, then why not give ourselves over to it? If we believe in it, it is so. We are not destined to think, to be, a certain way. We have choices. Believing in an ordered universe is not abdicating free will. It simply gives us a way of thinking about ourselves and learning to fit into that plan.

Despite our beginnings, or probably because of them, our lives are all perfect. They are perfect because what our lives are is what our lives are supposed to be.

In truth, since we are all part of the original collective energy, the big bang, then in reality there

is no separateness between events but simply a rec-
ognition of our individual paths, which originated in
that beginning.[7]

In order to see these motifs, we need to be able
to view ourselves from the perspective of the omnipotent
someone both watching us and being us. Without the
coloration of the internal, the external lacks great
significance. It is not an easy task to be able to divorce
ourselves from our closeness and to examine our
seeming happenstances and kismets, our synchro-
nicities and fates, critically and dispassionately enough
to draw meaning therefrom. It is necessary at times
to feel almost like a sieve, touching the matters that
pass through our lives but not attaching to them, for
if we begin to feel as though the events were in themselves the things that matter, we would lose the benefits
of the ability to let go.

This is what enlightenment in the Buddhist tradi-
tion would seem to mean.

> The observer is empty. Instead of a separate
> observer, we should say there is just *observing*.
> There is no one that hears, there is just hearing.
> There is no one that sees, there is just seeing.
> But we don't quite grasp that. If we practice hard
> enough, however, we learn that not only is the
> observer empty, but that which is observed is also
> empty....This is the final stage of practice; we
> don't need to worry about it....When nothing
> sees nothing, what do we have? Just the wonder
> of life. There is no one who is separated from

anything. There is just life living itself: hearing, touching, seeing, smelling, thinking. That is the state of love or compassion: not "It is I," but "It is Thou."[8]

Everything in our lives matters. There are no wrong turns or lost opportunities. We may regret some decisions we have made, but, in truth, no regrets are appropriate, for each decision is merely part of the continuum of our lives. Therefore, there are no mistakes, no failures, and, as a result, no need to fear our decisions. The gift is to be able to understand what each event means and how that event fits into the patterns, into the reasons, for our lives. And it appears that even those events that seem a diversion are really part of the perfection of our lives. We just have to know what to look for.

The difficulties we have in seeing ourselves in this fashion come because our views, limited as they are to the beginnings and endings of our own lives, are simply not long enough. It is as though we are seeing the world "through a narrow slit,"[9] an opening of perhaps sixty to seventy years when, in truth, our patterns have been emerging over eons, over several lifetimes — indeed, since the beginning of the universe. For example, in attempting to measure the distance of stars very far away from the Earth, astronomers can only use the platform of our planet to create a parallax from one side of our orbit around the sun to the other.

That is all we have.[10] Thus, because our parallax is so small relative to the great time and distances we need to examine, we are unable to see the patterns emerging any more than we can see the Earth change and the continents move. We know they do because science tells us they do, but we can only go on faith, not being able to be percipient observers. If we had a long enough perspective, all of the "but fors," all of the relationships, would be explained. As a result, we can only go on faith, trust, with respect to our own lives as well.

If we do see these patterns emerging when we examine our lives, we have the power of choice, to follow their perceived meaning. In doing so, we become free because we see how we are connected to the larger picture. This makes us feel safe because we find that there is no randomness, no need to control others, for all is as it is supposed to be.

AH! BUT WE DON'T!

The pressures we exert to resist finding this natural state are internal as well as external, although in truth the former are the true motivations for the latter. Out of fear of change, our inner beings create the appearance of being in control of any given circumstance so that we are perhaps able to convince ourselves that we are not the subject of change out of our control.

Certainty in life is hardly ever possible and yet we spend virtually all of our time seeking the feeling of security we believe it brings. We try to exclude everything that is different, which, by the very process of being different, we think creates uncertainty and insecurity. And all the while we are engaged in this search for certainty, we are paradoxically creating the very insecurity we seek to avoid. The more we search for security in the old, outside of ourselves, the less chance we ever have of finding it. The more we close ourselves to new ideas out of fear that we will come to realize we have been wrong, the less secure we will be. We can never work our way out of a problem by using the very same thinking that got us into the problem in the first instance.

We cling to the certainty of what we have, even though the same certainty does not bring us joy or happiness or satisfaction but only the certainty of more of the same. Better to know what is to be, no matter how tedious, boring, or horrible it may be, than the insecurity of not knowing what is coming.

> There can be no genuine deprecation of the present without the assured hope of a better future. For however much we lament the baseness of our times, if the prospect offered by the future is that of advanced deterioration or even an unchanged continuation of the present, we are inevitably moved to reconcile ourselves with our existence—difficult and mean though it may be.[11]

When we feel insecure, rather than open ourselves up to new ideas to escape from that feeling, we in fact regress and turn inward and backward toward more of the same. We refuse to face what we know to be true because to do so would require us to change. So we go on, with all of our pain, with all of our fear, because it is at least knowable.

When people in a marriage have difficulty in their relationship, they usually have a baby or buy new bedroom furniture.

We are resistant to change in any manner whatsoever, fearing the uncertainty of tomorrow. We do not understand that within any crisis lies the opportunity for change. It is unfortunate that fundamental change comes about only through crises. This is so because to alter our lives, to modify our thinking in basic, elemental ways, is scary stuff. We will not do so unless we are forced to, whether through death of loved ones, divorce, illness, war, or other such major moments. Without being flexible, without being unafraid to welcome the opportunity that the crisis brings, we regress to what we know, even though that brought about the crisis in the first instance. Certainty. Misery, to be sure, but certainty.

We want it to be different but we are unwilling to do what needs to be done to make it different. One cannot change without going through the process of changing. That process necessarily entails dangers, but those dangers are outweighed by the opportunities—outweighed, that is, if we allow those opportunities to rise to the surface and overcome the forces of resistance.

LETTING GO

The Tao helps us let go, if only a bit, of that to which we cling. It allows us to believe that we are safe if we ease up just a little.

Letting go—the simplest of ideas but the most difficult to live by. We have learned, through our lives, through past lives, through society, through family, through you-name-it, that attachments and holding on are what give us definition. What we have, who we are, the sorts of people and things we surround ourselves with, are the sum total of our beings, we are told. We are never taught that the methodology is far more important in determining what we mean and are about. We are only about growth. We must have the trust, the love, the insight in and for ourselves that allows us to give ourselves over to the process itself, trusting completely in its direction. If the significance of life is growth, then everything is part of that process and there can be, thus, no misfortunes. There may be sad events or happy ones, events that, no matter how strong our trust and faith may be, we must feel for and with, experiencing the sadness, the joy, the emotion of the time. But we learn that these are simply part of a larger series of life lessons and it is our job to look for them and learn from them.

By seeing the connections, by understanding the patterns, by feeling that we are a part of the universe, we can take the small step of letting go of the control we exert each day of our lives.

Knowing how we got here, knowing where we are going, not only allows us the luxury of feeling completely trusting about ourselves, but enables us to allow the same privilege to our lovers, for we understand completely that nothing in their exercise of their freedom can in any way infringe upon our own. Our destinies, while caught up inexorably with theirs, are still separate and apart. We can, each of us, enjoy our own levels of personal growth without feeling the need to restrict and contain the other's. This, in turn, gives us a feeling of peace about the seemingly important, but in reality unimportant, details of daily life that we might otherwise take too seriously and thus miss their meaning. When the perspective is growth, there can only be abundance. When there is abundance, there is no need for conflict, jealousy, feelings of competition, war.

THE WATCHER

Giving ourselves over to the universe allows us to turn off the inner voice, that voice which constantly looks over us, watches us, making sure we are in control. "Did I do that right or wrong?" "Should I feel bad about this?" "What about my love life?" It is this watcher, this censor, which creates the sense that we need to control things, for we feel that if we were just to "be," to co-exist with the universe, we could not trust ourselves; things would not come out the way we want them to. We have never learned to join, but instead have developed the checker of ourselves that categorizes and judges, takes notes and rates.

> When harmony comes not from subduing or peace from overpowering or quiet from silencing, then it is there. It is gone when struggling, lost when taking. It is given when receiving, filled when emptying.[12]

I return to the concept in Zen practice called "duality." This is separateness between our inner and outer selves. It is what keeps us from feeling integral with the universe. We are advised to turn off the checker, the watcher, and allow the seemingly two parts of ourselves to merge into one. "To stop your mind does not mean to stop the activities of mind. It means your mind pervades your whole body."[13]

> When we are embedded in life there is simply seeing, hearing, smelling, touching, thinking. . . . When we live this way there is no problem, there couldn't be. We are just *that*. . . .

When we aren't into our personal mischief, life is a seamless whole in which we are so embedded that there is no problem. But we don't always feel embedded because—while life is *just* life—when it seems to threaten our personal viewpoint we become upset, and withdraw from it. For instance, something happens that we don't like, or somebody does something to us we don't like, or our partner isn't the way we like.... They are based on the fact that suddenly life isn't just life (seeing, hearing, touching, smelling, thinking) anymore; we have separated ourselves and broken the seamless whole because we feel threatened. Now life is *over there*, and I am *over here*, thinking about it.[14]

This process is one of releasing the watcher and joining the outer and the inner voices and hearing only one. This merging of the seemingly two parts of ourselves is connecting with the universe. It is the goal. It has happened to me on only a few occasions, but for those sparse moments, I felt at one with everything. I felt connected. I felt at peace and open to everything.

Letting go is the ultimate task and requires us to separate ourselves from that which we perceive we know and to give ourselves over to the instant, which is unknowable since it is so transitory. Living in a place of not knowing can be very disconcerting unless we feel complete trust. It is the world of newness and of creativity. It is uncertainty, which is very exciting.

And so the circle is drawn, for we must let go of the outer voice, the checker, the watcher. We cannot achieve this breakthrough until we trust, and we cannot trust until we let go of control. We cannot let go of control unless we trust. The way out of this circle is to connect with the natural patterns that are clearly evident and, by this process, begin to feel that we are safe because we are connected to those processes.

Thus, it appears that the first and perhaps most important element to change in our lives is our resistance to change itself. In order to accomplish this, we must learn to let go of the need for control and to trust in our destinies. Crisis, and its inevitable consequence, change, is the universe speaking to us. It is the natural order of things screaming out for balance, for equilibrium, for a restoration of harmony, out of a situation that is fraught with imbalance, disequilibrium, and lack of harmony. In order to accomplish the letting go and the achieving of balance, we must learn that the universe is a harmonious place and that if we but learn to live in harmony with it, following the Tao, then we may be able to trust, to let go and find our way toward personal peace. In one sense, this seems very easy, and yet letting go and having faith is, in truth, *the* life lesson.

What is needed is the ability to feel secure enough about ourselves, individually and collectively, to let go of the old notions and open ourselves up to new thinking. What we must do is to turn off the wave machine and let the water find its own level, its equilibrium.

We really have no choice, for in the end, the natural processes will prevail no matter what we do.

> Stop the water and seize the river. Take hold of the air and possess the sky. Such foolish struggle. To seize the river ... become river. To possess the sky ... become sky.[15]

4

LOVE

I have often wished, for myself, that life were more like the movies and were accompanied by background music. That way, instead of being left to guess and worry about what was coming up next and live in fear of it, we would all know what the next scene in our lives was going to be just by listening.

LOVE, SIMPLICITY, AND OVERCOMING EGO ARE VERY much the same. True love does not hold but releases and gives freedom to another. True love cannot be complicated by rules, by control, by restrictions. If it cannot be felt and offered and accepted on its own basis, simply, then it is not true love. Simplicity also means balanced and harmonious, not restricted by external forces. It is simple because it is natural. By allowing ourselves to be loved by another, we must in the process be free of all ego. This also means being free of both external as well as internal restrictions on ourselves. It means being simple. It is the most difficult of ideas to understand and accept, and yet once understood and accepted, it is as simple as can be.

> I hold three treasures
> Close to my heart.
> The first is love;
> The next, simplicity;
> The third, overcoming ego.[1]

The essence of love is the ability to let go of ourselves, to free ourselves of the egocentrism that makes loving another and being in love more important than the underlying meaning of love. It is only when we learn to let go of ourselves and our *need* to be loved that we can find love, both from others and from the universe.

That which is kept will be lost. That which is lost will be kept. Have each other as if there cannot be keeping.[2]

Many of us go through life having a number of relationships in which we think we are experiencing love, but it turns out what we really are feeling is not love at all but need. It is need born from lack of love when we were children, which need we carry with us all of our lives unless we are able to free ourselves of it—all that grasping, all that clawing, all that holding on, all that pain. Hardly what we always thought love was supposed to be and yet that is all we know. Our frames of reference are limited by the remembrances of our past and our fears of the future. We are afraid of seeking the unknown, which is where true love takes us. Indeed, that is the essence of both the title and the book *Love Is Letting Go of Fear*, by Dr. Gerald Jampolsky.[3]

FEAR IS NOT LOVE

Our fear is that which comes from not being secure about ourselves and our places within the large scheme of things. If we knew how God thinks, everything else would be just details, to paraphrase Albert Einstein.

A great deal of our fear-based perspective comes from our individual notions of scarcity. We are taught scarcity, express and implied, from our birth. If one of us has, another must not have. There is not enough love, stuff, ideas, emotion to go around. Don't take the last cookie. How can you leave that food not eaten when the children in Europe are starving? How can you love without rules and limits? How can there be relationships without these rules?

For me, my parents' divorce when I was a child told me by implication that love was a scarce commodity. Afterwards, they were both unhappy, as was I. I learned that there was not enough love to make us all happy. That was the perspective that ruled me for decades. Its vestiges are still around.

Scarcity, which is the inevitable byproduct of lack of self-worth, comes to our adult lives as fear. Once we accept scarcity as a fact of our lives, then it is clear that we must continually fight to obtain abundance, without realizing that it can never come from outside. We fear losing our "stuff," our things, our love, and because we deem these to be scarce, we fight to hold on to them. We cling, we grasp until we destroy.

There is no scarcity. It exists only in our own minds and comes from our own creation. We are born into a world of abundance and then we imagine ourselves into a world of scarcity. We must first see abundance before our lives and our minds can become mirrors of the same.

At bottom, at the bottom-most of bottom lines,

is the truth that we are all the same. What we are in our lives is a product of what we were, or imagined ourselves to be, when we were children. That is the sum of our lives until we reach a point when we can recognize what we have been doing to ourselves and begin the process of freeing ourselves from these bonds of scarcity, either real or imagined. When our lack of self-worth becomes apparent to us, we have the choice of either letting go of this image or, what seems more common, projecting our faults and lacks onto others and foisting the blame onto them. Doing the latter convinces us that we are right, they are wrong, and, in the process, helps us try to cover up for our own lack of self-worth.

The Tao teaches abundance, since the universe is a connected whole. There are no shortages of anything when we see the world in this fashion.

But instead, we all operate out of fear. What is all this fear about? It seems to be a generalized, ill-defined, not very directed fear. Most of us who have a deep, abiding fear of a particular evil have had no actual contact with it, but we have been told it is evil and that it threatens us and so we respond, like so many salivating dogs, to the bait. It is the arch-evil that must be guarded against and fought in all of its manifestations. Everything that is not opposed to it must be it in disguise and must be viewed with alarm and fear. But asked to identify the fear, we are struck with the seeming illogic and irrationality of it all, for it is not really identified as creating an actual danger to us. Often it is a fear that has been told to us by others, by parents, friends, enemies, the media, governments. It has been told so often that it has taken on the character of being very real, even though it is imaginary or, at best, overly exaggerated and not worthy of the large measure of importance we attach to it.

We fear death and dying. But if we believe in another perspective, say the continuity of life, then this can ease our fears. The choice of belief systems is up to us. We fear being wrong. But if we believe that everything we do is merely part of our growth, then there is no wrong. The choice of belief systems is up to us.

In terms of love, it is in part a fear of losing our existence. If we fall in love and need the other person too much, if we define ourselves as being part of a team instead of simply as us, we fear that losing the relationship would mean loss of ourselves. That comes from the perception of scarcity, since we feel that if the relationship ends, so will we.

We also fear the unknown. It is why we create idols, or gods, or even the Tao. We try to make sense out of the universe so that we can feel we can control our destinies. We are deeply fearful of letting someone get truly close, irrespective of how much we say that

that is what we want. It is frightening to have an open soul. Thus, when we love we exercise tight control. Few actually learn to be loved.

When I walked on the Great Wall in China it struck me that this real wall was about keeping fear out. Our imaginary walls do the same.

It is the fear of separation that keeps us separated. It is the fear of loss and its pain that keeps us from making the complete commitment to the relationship that is the essence of love. The ability to feel has nothing to do with the need to hold. When we cling, it is out of a sense that if we let go, somehow we will lose a part of us. And indeed, that generally is so because we are not complete without the other. We need the other to make us whole so that if the other leaves, we are in fact incomplete. So we hold on, trying to keep the other from doing or thinking anything that we feel will jeopardize the relationship and us. And the more we try to make that other ours, the more the other struggles to be free. And the more the other struggles to be free, the more we tighten our grasp. And neither of us knows what is going on until it is over.

Islands and walls look different at different times, but they all have the same function. Most of our fear stems from our childhood, when we developed our perceptions that created the basis for that fear.[4] If the love we were given was not what we wanted, or was otherwise perverted, if only in our minds, then we, at that early stage, set the framework for our later fears about closeness and our abilities to be loved and lovable. If, according to our perceptions at that age, we felt that our parents did not think we were worth loving, then we simply carry that perception into our later lives, however misplaced and irrelevant it may be twenty, thirty, or forty years later. We have failed to grow if we continue to allow our self-concept to be ruled by what was but no longer is. It becomes self-fulfilling, for we find reasons to fail in love. If we were open in our personal lives, we would have nothing to fear from others whose fear is based on the same things as ours. We are afraid of each other because we are afraid of ourselves. But instead of acknowledging this mutual fear, we retreat and treat the other as an enemy. And they do the same thing and we do the same thing and so on and so on.

When we act out of fear, out of concern that if the relationship changes we will lose something, we usually turn out to be right. Fear is not the basis for any partnership and, in the end, is its undoing. Fear, leading to control, grasping, stifling growth, all are negative emotions that somehow we trick our minds into thinking are positive. We call it love but it is not love. When we are unable to let go, when we feel that we are entitled to something, when we feel that we must make it work whatever the cost, when we are inflexible to and struggle against apparent change, when we fail to understand that an ending is just as important as a beginning, that is when we experience real heartache. Maybe it takes the form of illness—cancer, heart attack, or the like. Maybe it is in the form of depression, when we feel dissatisfied about reaching our goals. It is in fact all the same, and so we are both the process and the result.

The same thoughts are expressed in Zen practice.

> How much of our love is genuine depends on how we practice with false love, which breeds in the emotion-thought of expectation, hopes, and conditioning.[5]

When we expect something out of love, out of our relationship with another, then we will surely be disappointed, for loving means having no expectations. When we want the other to be a certain way, to fulfill certain of our expectations, and he or she does not, love turns to disappointment in us.

Expectations come as a result of our attempts to control the world, to make it come out the way we want it to. We try to control the other person. Instead of always trying to get what we want, we must learn to let go and seek from the world what we need.

We feel we must find our security in love, only

to discover, if not to admit, that we can never be secure about ourselves by defining that security in terms of the love of another.

Love is totally the opposite of that which most of us have felt in the past. The positive, freeing sensation of love comes from being secure in ourselves and not feeling threatened by our partner. To feel complete by ourselves is liberating. To know that, whatever comes of the relationship and this particular partner, we will still be us is freeing.

Before love can truly exist with another, it must first exist for ourselves. It is only when we realize that the most positive form of love is born out of self-love first that we truly feel the emotion.

> If we cannot love ourselves, where will we draw our love for anyone else? People who do not love themselves can adore others, because adoration is making someone else big and ourselves small. They can desire others because desire comes out of a sense of inner incompleteness, which demands to be filled. But they cannot love others, because love is an affirmation of the living, growing being in all of us. If you don't have it, you can't give it.[6]

LOVING IS DIFFERENT FROM BEING LOVED

We find it to be much easier to love than to be loved. To love another is something we can learn by watching actors in movies or reading great romances. The role models are freely available, even though not everyone does it equally well. There is, however, no place we can go to learn how to allow ourselves to be loved.

Allowing ourselves to be loved is very much a different matter from loving. It is not simply the other side of the same coin. Allowing ourselves to be loved by another requires us, from the outset, to be completely out of control and vulnerable. It requires us to break down all the walls that, for so many years of our lives, we have struggled to erect to keep us from feeling the very thing we say we want to feel. The Tao calls it "ego." It means that we must expose our complete selves to our lover, our mate, for without such total openness what is being called love is something else but it is not love. If each partner is simply loving the other but is not in turn allowing himself or herself to be loved by the other, then no intimacy is being shared. We each might just as well be loving a mirror.

Loving another means being in control. We select the terms on which we shall give our love. We can woo, we can wine, we can dine. We can give gifts when it suits our fancy, or our needs, to do so. We set the agenda and we can give as little or as much of ourselves as we choose, for it is we who determine how far we will go to express love. From the perspective of the male, loving a woman is a form of machismo, a male-oriented expression. We grow up believing that it is expected of us and, if we are fortunate, most of us "fall in love" on at least several occasions in our lives. If we have never been in love, we seem to feel we are unnatural and out of place in society. Even during the most romantic of times, however, we are still in control. Of her and ourselves.

For men, allowing ourselves to be loved involves letting go of the male ego, the *yang*, and allowing the female, the *yin*, side of our personalities to become exposed. This is very difficult for most men to accomplish and comes only with significant personal growth. In our masculine-dominated world, the male perspective prevents us from acknowledging that we also have a female side to ourselves. To acknowledge this female side of our personalities is deemed a sign of weakness and is seen as anti-masculine. It is the equivalent of being dependent, and men do not like to seem dependent.[7] If we need another to make us whole, then we are vulnerable to that other. If we need another, then we must control the other so that we feel secure through that control. But we never get to that place of security because we know, in truth, that at any moment our control over the other could cease. But rather than recognize this, we overlay additional means of control in our attempt to create security out of insecurity.

Traditionally, men did not recognize the existence of female aggression. They needed to maintain an image of her as weak in order that they could deny their own dependency needs and to see themselves as strong.[8]

But like the *yin* and the *yang* itself, each of us contains both aspects of love. We each are both male and female, if we have the freedom to allow them to become exposed. "As man or woman we must come to terms with ourselves and our sexual counterpart, not only in a physical way but also in a philosophical and aesthetic way."[9]

Women, as often as men, find it easier to love than to be loved. They are, as often as their male counterparts, accused of holding themselves back and not letting the other in. Both men and women, often unconsciously, hold themselves close, unwilling to give all, because to do so would make them vulnerable to being hurt, to having their old baggage brought up to them again.

In our attempts to control the outside, we forget that change never occurs there but only here. If we wish the other to change, we must first change ourselves. Instead, we attempt to coerce and force the other into fundamental alterations of himself or herself while all the while pretending that we are loving to the core. We all want the other to be the one who changes.

In fact, we never really are in control of our lives. That at a given moment we seem to be happy, that things are going the way we wish them to, is no indication that in fact we have made them come out that way but simply reflect the synchronicity of the moment. Lives have a way of changing instantly and in that process getting beyond our control. Lives change radically in an instant in time—a simple telephone call, a word from a lover, or such. (Again it is important to understand that such a concept is no refutation of the idea of personal responsibility. We have the choice to believe as we do.)

Being in control implies something static and stable. If we are in control, we feel we can make predictions and have dreams. We search for signs of this stability but, except for short periods, it appears that there is no stability in life. What we find, if we step out of the substance for a moment, is that it is a process, one which leads to ever-changing levels of pain, growth, happiness, pain again, and so on.

Being in control also leads to sterility, to fear of what caused pain at an earlier time, and to the building of walls to keep out anything that could hurt as much as that did. Isolation and control are much the same. Not being open is the common thread. We maintain constant vigil against any signs that we are coming unraveled or that another may have an impact on our lives that might hurt later on.

In order to allow ourselves to be loved by another, we must first have come to the place in our lives where we allow ourselves to love ourselves. When we have grown to such a degree that we feel totally trusting in our destinies, our lives, our God, our selves, then we have come to that place. We know that nothing can take away from us our fundamentally significant love of us. It is at such a time that we can let go of the need for control, for there is, in fact, nothing to control. It is all perfect, no matter what it is, for it is as it was supposed to be. Since we are part of everything, there is nothing to be lost.

The opposite of control is trust. We begin to learn to love ourselves by giving ourselves over to this trust. To be able to trust ourselves to a process larger than ourselves is the ultimate peace of mind. To cede our power to this instinct, once recognized and found to be true, is to give ourselves over to faith and to the belief that all will turn out for the best, if we know what to look for. To have this sense of trust, however, comes only from giving up control. It takes much strength to do so. The paradox is that the ability to trust comes only from the pain of not having trusted in the first instance. Only when we have tried to control and when we have been unsuccessful and that has resulted in deep hurt can we even begin the process of learning from the hurt. It bears repeating that we grow only out of crisis.

It is ironic that the very process of letting go and giving up control is also the process of taking on personal responsibility for ourselves. We are, by doing so, saying to ourselves that we, not something out there, not something over which we feel we have control, is determining our destinies. We are making the decisions.

LETTING GO ... AGAIN

If we had the ability to trust in ourselves, in our destinies, in the Tao, in the natural order of things, we could then let go enough to find the true meaning of love. If we felt, in our souls, that we were connected to the universe and thus everything that was to be would be, we would be able to let go of the fear that keeps us from doing just that.

Internal peace, peace in the form of love of others, begins with love of the self. We cannot begin to love another until we love ourselves. What we experience, in the name of love but, in truth, merely want or need, is not love at all. Love means letting each other be free, and we cannot let the other be free if we ourselves are in chains.

It turns out, after much growth, usually born out of pain from failed relationships, that being out of control and being vulnerable to another is the single greatest security we can have in any relationship.

A seeming paradox but, in truth, no conflict at all. This sort of vulnerability comes not from weakness but rather from strength. It is not the sort of vulnerability that tells us, in our deepest souls, that we are in danger from the other but one that tells us we have come so far in our growth that we can believe totally in ourselves, that we can, as a consequence, allow ourselves to become exposed to another, and that there is nothing to fear from such exposure.

We get this security from allowing ourselves to be one with the natural process. Then we are not vulnerable, because there is no outside to attack us. It is only when we hide behind our walls from where we feel invulnerable to such harm that we have less concern about inflicting the very harm on others that we mortally fear. We are protected on our island that gives us shelter from pain. We fail to realize that that self-same island is the source of much pain and insecurity, for we know the other's island may be giving that one the same sense of security, however false it is.

HAPPINESS COMES FROM FREEING OURSELVES OF FEAR

Happiness, loving, caring, feeling about a situation in a positive manner, looking at the world without fear are all about the same thing. In each of our lives, we truly can create our own reality, a reality that can be negative or positive. Loving another, loving ourselves, is part of that reality. When we tell ourselves, when we convince ourselves, that we are ready to open up to love, love may come our way—not a negative thing that passes for love, but a deeply caring, nurturing experience. But it can only happen when we feel good enough about ourselves to allow ourselves the vulnerability of love.

When we are unable to feel love, to feel caring, indeed to feel happiness, we will also always be right. We will somehow find a way to prove ourselves to be right. Better to be right than happy. Maybe being right, no matter how miserable we are, is a form of happiness to some. Some people, for reasons known to them only, are unable to accept goodness, fun, pleasure, and success in their lives. They have grown up with such a fear of happiness, such a terror of having, that when they get what they feel they want, they destroy themselves for having it. They are unable to see the future unhampered by the chains of their past.

Some of us come to our adult lives with a deep sense of guilt, feeling that if we have things, if we have happiness, if we meet the right person, if our careers take off, we are unworthy and undeserving of pleasure and we must be punished for it. And when we cannot find punishment enough in the outer world, we find ways to punish ourselves inwardly. Some of us turn to drugs or food, some to drink, some to physical abuse of our bodies, all in an attempt to deprive ourselves of what we have but feel that we do not deserve.

Perhaps our parents were poor and struggled in order to give to us. This can breed a sense of guilt, as though it were our fault that we went to college, for example. Perhaps the parents themselves were not happy in the marriage but stayed together "for the sake of the children," which never works. Perhaps it was other events that, perceived from our child's perspective, produced a feeling of unworthiness. Whatever the cause, it reflects itself in our outlook in terms of ourselves and our relationship with others. We undermine ourselves for the sake of being able to say: "See, I really didn't deserve it for all that I did! I really am not a good person."

Some of us have adopted an approach to living that continually results in our being injured, hurt, shot down, demoralized, defeated, an approach that regularly causes untold harm to ourselves, is self-destructive, and generally does nothing to help us achieve a peaceful, loving life. We should ask what motivates us to continue holding such a clearly unproductive viewpoint. Perhaps we would conclude that, notwithstanding our statements to ourselves and to others that we wanted love, because of our need to continue to be the victim, we continue to undermine our own goals so that we can continue to prove to ourselves that we are not worthy enough to have love. It is a well-accepted myth that it is easier to be a victim than to be a free person.

The truly free are free enough to try something new when it is apparent that the old is not working. There is no gain in holding on simply because we are afraid of the untried. The unfree, the afraid, the weak, those pretending to be strong are so scared of life that they are willing to persist with the old, duping themselves into believing that, even though it is not working now, if only they try harder, if only they close their eyes tighter, someday it will work. They never define love, nor do they envision what love will look like, because they have no true perspective of love, never having given love a chance to surface.

We are, however, in denial. We change therapists. We change friends. We change spouses. We seek out only those who play the sycophant to us, give us sympathy, and tell us to persevere because we are right in our approach. Generally, on close examination, those whom we befriend are equally afraid, equally self-destructive, equally unable to see the proverbial forest for the trees. Unless some miracle occurs or we are absolutely forced by circumstances to waken to our disastrous plight, we die in the state of unrest that our mental sickness created for us.

It is the same personal denial, by the way, when

looked at in the macroworld, that keeps us from accepting our collective plight. It keeps us from changing, because it is painful to recognize that we have been misled and are in turn misleading ourselves to continue the paths we have chosen when it is clear that they are leading to death. We are in denial about war, but we know no other recourse. We are in denial about exhaustion of our resources, but we refuse to give up anything because it is the things that we feel keep us secure. We are in denial about our bondage to our particular ism and, as a result, we enslave others to believe in our ism so that differences do not arise.

It takes a lot of growing to feel good enough about ourselves to allow the other to be as free as we would like to be ourselves. It takes a great deal of personal strength to give the other the freedom to be whatever that other wants to be without feeling threatened by freedom. It takes knowing that without freedom for both, neither will survive the relationship. To give the other the room to grow, to experience things that may not be to our liking and that may even cause the relationship to change, takes a very positive feeling about ourselves. With this kind of freedom, the love can continue to grow, although it may take a different direction. Without it, there is no growth at all.

This is the Taoist principle of "non-attachment." It does not mean indifference to the other but rather holding on to a love very loosely so that the loved one is free to go and free to be. It means knowing that should the relationship end, we would still be whole.

Being able to let go of the fear, of the control, to believe that the universe is a harmonious place when we live in harmony with it gives us the ability to trust. Being able to trust, we are able to let go of the need to control our lovers, our friends, our enemies, if you will. We see everyone as part of the same universe, and if everyone let go of the need to control and fear, then no one would be seen as the attacker or the one under attack.

The Tao teaches that everything exists in relationship to everything else. If all is in harmony, in balance, in equilibrium, then simple, almost arithmetical thinking tells us that when one side of an equation changes, the other side must change as well to accommodate the first change in order to maintain the equality. Accordingly, if we wish the other to change, we can either force that change or simply change how we are. Changing how we look at the world, our perspective can cause the other person in the relationship to change as well.

By attuning ourselves with the universe, with the Tao, by seeing ourselves as part of it, we can see where we are going. Perhaps then we can feel that life indeed is accompanied by background music.

5

HOW DO WE CHANGE?

We grow when we practice daily the process of growing.

Having said everything that has come before, how might we change? How do we go about the process of understanding as much of the universe as we are given to understand and letting go of the desperate need we have for control so we can go with the natural forces? How do we learn to trust enough in ourselves so that we can let go? How do we recognize the Tao when we feel it?

> The Tao is like a well:
> used but never used up.[1]

The Tao will give you only what you give to it. It is not the answer but a way to the answer. The long path to love begins with the first step, which starts at your own door. Love is the expression of a person at peace with himself or herself. To get to the point where we can give as well as receive love, we must find ourselves first. Thus, the path to love begins with understanding ourselves. So this chapter will not deal with how to find a date for Saturday night, or a mate, or what to say, how to dress, and so on. Those may all follow once you know yourself. Finding love, as opposed to romance, is about discovering roots.

I wish I had some rules, some guidelines, some checklists that, if you followed them, would, like some magical potion, be able to sweep away your fears. I have none. What I have are merely some suggestions, because, like the Tao itself, it is up to each of us to fill our well according to our own lives. And yet these suggestions apply to each of us, for when we pare away the various scenarios of our individual lives, our issues are pretty much the same. They revolve around self-love or the lack of it and how we feel about ourselves. At the root we are all very much alike, but we have different symptoms so that we do not bore each other to tears at parties.

We grow not because one day we awaken and realize all that we need to understand and are, at once, at peace with the world. Enlightenment, for that is what we are speaking of, takes lifetimes to achieve. All we can hope to do in any given lifetime is to begin, or continue, the process. We grow when we take little baby steps and see that we are safe, thus finding a little more courage to take somewhat larger steps the next time. We grow when our pain is too much to bear and we force ourselves, or are by circumstances forced, to act differently.

All of these processes may, of necessity, involve seeking professional assistance from therapists, psychologists or others, and you should seek them out as you need to, for neither this book nor any other book provides all that you need. But nothing and no one will help us change unless we are ready to change. There is no therapy, there is no philosophy, that will be useful unless we are committed to ourselves. The pain of stagnating, of being unhappy, must be so great that we must be willing to try anything just to be relieved of it—anything, including something new. Having faith requires us to live our faith and not merely speak of it nor even intellectually understand it. It requires us to *be* our faith even in the face of "real world" daily stuff that gets in the way. We cannot become one with the Tao, one with ourselves, until we take steps to purify and simplify our lives, to cleanse them of the spiritual and emotional dualities that separate us from merely being.

EXAMINE YOUR PAIN

The pain is the original pain of childhood. It remains with us into our adult lives until something forces us to examine that pain and make changes so that we no longer are ruled by it. It involves discovering first the information and then the emotion surrounding our parental relationships at that time. Remember that the Tao teaches us that it is pain that gives meaning to no pain, and thus it is pain that leads to growth. In one sense, the pain you must work out is truly a blessing, for it is the engine of change.

I have always thought that, with today's technology, videotaping births is a wonderful way of dispelling our initial myths. Being able to see ourselves at the moment of entry into this world seems a good way of assuring ourselves that, at least at that moment, we were safe. It could save thousands of hours of trying to figure out what we never can be certain of without having been there. If you are contemplating having children, you might want to try this.

If you have siblings, compare notes. Talk to your brother or sister who shared the same experiences as you but who perhaps saw things from a different point of view. It could be a great awakening to see how he or she understood those same events. Your differing perspectives might shed light on whatever misunderstandings you each developed. There are of course at least two sides to every story and hearing the other one sometimes clears it all up.

Most of us never talk to our parents about our fears or our perceptions from our youth. It is as though we feel they would never understand anyway. Why hurt them with old news? But what seems the simplest thing to do is to talk to them, ask what happened, get their side of the story. This too may clear things up. In the process, you may get to know them better. Waiting serves no purpose at all and should they die without you having heard what they had to say, you may carry the burden alone for the rest of your life.

If it is too painful to speak with them directly, try writing them a letter, even if you do not mail it. Merely putting into written form all of your pain may make the vagaries of your fears diminish. What you will be doing in both circumstances is cleaning up old and unfinished business, and it is this stuff, when it lies around in our minds decade after decade, that becomes the compost fuel for sad thoughts.

Getting to the roots of the issues is of great importance. We can never know the true "story" of our lives unless we know how it started. Seek out professional help if you need to, for it is especially important here.

TALK TO YOURSELF

This hurting child, which each of us has within ourselves, needs comforting. It is you who need the comforting, but if you talk to this child, say how much you love this child, say he or she is safe, that may help you feel safe. Most of us do not feel safe because we did not feel safe as children. Hug yourself. Begin to treat this child inside of you as you would want to be treated yourself. You would not want to abuse the child, nor stuff the child full of alcohol or drugs or food. Take care of the child.

This helped me. I found a photograph of myself as a child, one that reflected my internal state of fear. If you look carefully, those fears were apparent even then and the lens knows how to spot them. When I was going on a vacation, a time of joy, I took the photograph with me and let my little child have as much fun on the trip as I was having. I let the child know that it was all right to have fun, to enjoy, to explore and to not fear the universe. We both had a great time.

It is vitally important that we become more accepting of ourselves. Our search for perfection is merely our trying to right the perceived inadequacies we feel we have, and those, as we have seen, depend on our perspective from childhood. But the more we search for perfection, the more we build into our current perceptions the basis for continued self-deprecation. We will always make mistakes and if we view each such mistake as proof that we are not worthy, we will always lose. Ease up. Please.

When you achieve a breakthrough, however small, reward yourself. Buy something nice for yourself. Tell yourself how wonderful you are because of what you have done.

EXPLAIN YOUR FEARS CONCRETELY

As I have said, most of us have only this vague, generalized sense of dread about what we fear. We have never really tried to picture how these fears will be manifested in real life. What is it that you really think will happen to you if you let go and break a pattern or two? Will you die or fall off the Earth? Make a list of what you fear and what you fear will happen to you. Perhaps the written expression of these fears and their consequences may add some rationality, some logic, to the emotionalism that is the fear.

Just as we cannot fully let go of any logic in trying to come up with a new way of thinking because logic and rational thought help us relate to the real world, this same rationality and logic can help us break our patterns and addictions to self-defeating behavior. Seeing them, speaking about them, writing them down forces us to get concrete about our fears and may help us see them as irrational in many instances.

Explain your fears to someone else, as well as to yourself. Find a good therapist if that is what you need. If you choose a friend, choose wisely but give it a try. Being open is the best way of getting another to be open. Remember, we all want the other to do the changing. But in order to get the other to change, we must first change.

In this process of exploration, try being alone more. Set aside a regular period when you can do so. Do not crowd yourself with crowds. Many of us fear being with ourselves and yet it is difficult to grow when we are surrounded by people, events, things that easily distract us. The work we must do is so hard that it is natural to seek any excuse not to do it. Being alone takes away those excuses.

Finally, be honest with yourself. Many of us have never been honest with ourselves and so we do not know what is the truth any longer. But you must peel away the layers of deceit that you have built up over the decades and begin to seek the deepest truths. Being open with another is impossible if you have not been open with yourself.

Examine Your Patterns

We tend to repeat our behavior because to do so is a form of control. We believe that if we do not venture too far from what we know, no matter how boring, hurtful, painful it is, at least we know what to expect. We do this even if we do not know we are doing it. How many of us have had one bad relationship after another, with a person who was almost exactly like our prior mate? These patterns also tend to be repetitions of how our parents treated us when we were children. We marry or get involved with mates who treat us like our parents did. We may hate it but, again, it is a form of control since at least we can predict.

Our patterns are repetitions of what we believed worked for us when we were children. In truth, they did not work even then, but we, being children, had no other choice except to keep on keeping on. Now that we are adults, however, we have many choices, although most of us limit our choices because diversity is scary.

If we grew up believing we were not worthy, we fall into relationships that prove that to us over and over again. We unconsciously find unhappiness because it tells us that we do not deserve happiness.

Once having examined your patterns, take some small steps to break them. Finding a new environment requires us to get out of the auto-pilot into which we fall when we perpetuate our patterns. Drive home a different way from work. Drink your coffee in another room. Eat lunch or dinner at a different time. Go to a place you have never been before. Try doing it alone. Do whatever you do differently from the way you did it yesterday. If you need help, find support from others, whether professionals or friends.

ACT AS IF YOU BELIEVED

One way to break this repetitive system is to act as if you felt good about yourself. Try simple things first toward breaking a self-destructive pattern in your life and see whether anything bad happens to you. Open yourself up to the cashier at the market. Smile and see if you get a smile back. It is frightening, but it is the process of changing, and that is what each of us fears the most.

After all, the best part about meeting someone new is that you can be anything you want to be. There is simply no need to carry with you into this new relationship anything about your past or who you were yesterday. You are in no fashion obligated to retain your poor self-image, nor are you required to replay your old self for this new person. You can be, in a very real sense, as free as you want to be, for the person you meet today has no way of knowing your background. He or she does not know whether you had a happy or an unhappy childhood. That person is unaware of whether yesterday you saw the world out of love or hate or whether you fear tomorrow or look forward to it with great glee and excitement. To each new person you encounter, you are a *tabula rasa*, a clean slate. It follows that who you are to the world today can be and simply is a function of your own freedom or lack thereof. You have the total and complete ability to be free, and in the process of being free to free yourself of the burdens of your past. After all, they have absolutely no relevance to your today, so just act as if you were strong and confident. Pretend.

Of course, most of us just act like we did yesterday, thereby perpetuating the bad self-image we had of ourselves then. We squander this wonderful opportunity to pretend that we are something we really are but believe we are not. What happens is that if you do let go and act as if you were self-assured, the other person reacts accordingly, because we are all in a relationship with everyone else. So then you are reinforced and get the courage to try it again, and so on. And this new person you meet just assumes that this is who you are and so, at least to him or her, you are that way.

Try small changes at first. Make a list of what you would like to be and feel, given the total freedom to be just that way. We all need a vision. Make it concrete. Start with changes that are achievable so that you get "wins" right from the beginning. With each win, you develop the confidence to move toward the next one.

This is one way to build trust, in yourself and in others. Once we practice these new ideas and find that we are still safe, we begin to accept ourselves as being secure. Once that happens, we can open ourselves up to newer and more daring experiments in terms of letting go even further.

SEE THE LARGER PICTURE

Remember the "but for" notion? By seeing the larger patterns in our lives, by feeling that there is a destiny being explained by these connections, we begin to feel that there is an order to the universe into which we fit. Step back and make a list of connections, starting from today and working backward. How did you get this job? How did you meet this person or that? How is it that you are living where you are and not over there?

I mentioned earlier that the Tao speaks to us through the myriad of signs that are given to us to read, to hear, and to see. The Tao helps us attune ourselves to those signs. We have all had them. Some call it instinct. Some claim to have had a religious experience. But a sign can be as simple as a busy signal telling us not to talk to this person at this time. Whatever you call it, those signs are there for us to read. When you want something and it is not happening the way you want it to happen, it is the universe telling you to back off and let go. What will happen will happen.

Learn to read these signs. They are your entry into the "letting go" club. They are there but you must be open to see them. They are like the children's puzzles where you must find the ten animals in the forest, but the picture is drawn in such a way that you must think conceptually and creatively, looking upside down and askew to see them. They are there but you must lose your mind to see them.

You will have to let go of all that you feel you control in order to act on your heart. The Tao is really our instincts speaking to us. Most of us overrule ourselves because we do not trust enough to do anything our heart tells us. But if you believe in yourself, if you believe in God, if you believe in what the Tao tells, you can have the courage to let go.

EXAMINE YOUR CONTRIBUTIONS

Since our personal growth can be a springboard for our awareness of the need to heal the planet, it can also be true in reverse. Feeling safe in the world is the goal in order to let go of the control that fights the natural forces, so working to make the Earth a safer place to live is part of the solution. See how your life fits into saving the planet. Do you recycle? How many biodegradable products do you use? Do you participate in community efforts to make others aware of the need to work with and not against nature?

The contributions do not have to be monumental on a planetary scale. Do what feels comfortable for you. I once had a student who attended a class that ended late in the evening and she had a thirty-mile drive home. When I asked what the class had learned about peace at the conclusion of the semester, she told me that for her, peace meant that she did not speed when she drove home at night.

Feeling connected to the planet in this fashion may help you believe that you have taken some measure of responsibility for the world and your contribution to it. This feeling of personal responsibility for your conduct is empowering. It may help emancipate your other feelings of being a victim. We can change ourselves by doing for others since in doing so, we take ourselves out of our egocentric condition and move into the larger arena where the self has to deal with issues that are out of our control because they are happening to others.

Teach your children, if you have any, about these ideas even if you have not yet fully absorbed them for yourself. We are never totally enlightened and if we all waited until we were to pass the word along, we would get nowhere. Give your children alternative ideas. Tell them that it is all right to think differently from you. Allow them free expression. If you act as if you believed, you can give your children a role model to follow. Do not be hypocritical. Tell them you are trying, you are growing, experimenting. But follow through on what you tell them. Children can learn to accept change when they see their parents changing.

Speak to your children about God and love and spirituality, about what you believe. Do not force it upon them with rituals and rules. Let them see that you act on your beliefs and they can then be free to find their own way into the spiritual universe.

Be open with your children about the changes you are going through. Stoicism, keeping a stiff upper lip, is nonsense. Children can sense the pain, so be forthright about it. It may teach them that pain is natural and they may learn not to resist it but allow it free expression. It may open them up to change as they grow and they may, in turn, pass that openness along to their children and so on. It is by this process that the world changes.

MEDITATE AND DO AFFIRMATIONS

As amorphous as this suggestion may seem (and I hate it when I read it in "how to" books as well), there is a good deal of validity to the process of going inward. We must learn to feel the presence of the universe, of God, if you will, inside each of us in order to feel connected. That presence makes itself known in the heart. We can feel it only when we get quiet and be with ourselves alone.

Doing affirmations, telling yourself repeatedly that you are safe, that you are a good person, that you deserve abundance in the world, that you are worthy of love, may, over time, become part of your belief system. We do create our own reality, and our reality is based on what we perceive the world to be about. Positive, affirming statements to ourselves help us create that reality.

Find some alternative philosophy to follow. Learn about astrology or Eastern religions or anything else that opens you up to other ideas that you have not allowed in.

GET A PUPPY

If your circumstances permit, buy a puppy, or, better still, save one from the pound or local shelter. Get down on the floor and play with and hug and love your puppy. Rub its belly. Take care of it, and you may soon find that you can give, and get, love free from all the fears that come with its human counterpart. You may find no restraints-mushy-fun and, mostly, safe love—love that will never come with strings, love that does not care about who you are, what you have, what you look like, love that may open you up to what love should be about, the kind of love that God intended for us all to share. It may give you a standard by which to seek other love.

ARE YOU DOING WHAT YOU LOVE TO DO?

I have always told my children, when they were teenagers thinking about what they wanted for themselves first to figure out what you love to do and then figure out how to make a living at it. There are people making a living at things they love. Our society teaches us just the opposite. Find a career: doctor, lawyer, accountant. Never mind whether you like it or not. Be secure. Do what you like on Tuesday nights or on the weekend. This is stupid for many reasons but, relative to this book, it is stupid because it deprives us of love in a major part of our lives. Our work, how we spend the majority of our time, affects how we spend the rest of our time, and the quality of our work affects the quality of the rest of our time. If we dread Mondays through Fridays, we will not be open to relationships with others during that time or even on the weekends. We will be miserable and take it out on others with whom we associate. We will be closed to love.

We all get caught up in this pattern of finding a job and ignore what we love doing. It is extremely difficult to give up the safety of a steady salary or income in favor of a dream. But if we do not dream, then we die.

> If one listens to the faintest but constant suggestions of his genius, which are certainly true, he sees not to what extremes, or even insanity, it may lead him; and yet that way, as he grows even more resolute and faithful, his road lies. The faintest assured objection which one healthy man feels will at length prevail over the arguments and customs of mankind. No man ever followed his genius till it misled him.[2]

All this may seem a very nondirect approach to love but it is, in truth, the most direct route. Love may come to you when you are open to accept love. You can be open only when you open yourself to yourself. These suggestions are just some of the ways you may be able to break the rigidity that has bound us for eons and has kept us from finding love.

6

CONCLUSION

In the end, we are both the substance of our own perspectives as well as the process for changing them. Nothing will change until we change, for we are the somethings that must change. We are our own lack of love.

It bears repeating: We can change our futures by changing our minds. We define our belief systems about how the world operates by the choices we make, and, indeed, many of these choices are unconscious, having come from our past without any direct input from us. We can change even these unconscious choices by opening ourselves to new ideas that intentionally upset our belief systems. We do so when the pain of continuing with them overwhelms us. We have limited our minds even in the face of the unlimited possibilities that the universe affords us. We have done so out of fear of the very possibilities we seek.

> In moments of darkness and pain
> remember all is cyclical.
> Sit quietly behind your wooden door:
> Spring will come again.[1]

We continue to believe that we are here and that the rest of the seemingly objective real world is floating out there in some undefined place. This separation produces fear of loss and so we hold on tight to what we feel we have, and the tighter we hold on, the less secure we feel.

We fear freedom. We have never really been free, most of us, and so the concept is alien to us. We understand freedom of the vote and freedom of the marketplace because those ideas are objective and concrete. But we truly do not understand what it means to be free. Freedom 'comes from inside and has little to do with the outside. The outside can be as free as we, on the inside, allow ourselves to make it.

Because we fear freedom in our individual lives, we must restrict freedom for those whom we would love, lest the freedom they have be seen as a threat to our freedom.

The thought of a new idea, a different way of looking at the world, never enters our minds. Fresh approaches are quickly made to seem foolish, for they will not work in a week or a month. Without the promise of immediate results, like aspirin, we refuse to try anything. So we plod along, decrying our state, but fearing change and thus perpetuating our own lack of love.

Granted, there are times when all seems out of our control, beyond the capacities of most of us to effectuate any sort of change no matter how well-meaning we are. It seems sometimes that changing ourselves is even more difficult than changing the world. We are gripped by inertia, which is the scientific principle that a body at rest tends to stay at rest unless acted upon by a force. We remain inert because the sheer overwhelming magnitude of our task keeps us inert, at least until our pain grows so deep that we must do something.

And yet, a great deal has changed. I have changed. I have been changed by the very process of writing and communicating to you the ideas that I have set forth here. I have been changed because I found that I could have a voice, however small and perhaps ineffective in the larger scheme of things it may be. I have changed because the very act of gaining this voice was an empowering process for me. Change is both a substantive event as well as the process of working for that substantive event. It is both looking for actual changes in the real world and going through the process of trying to effectuate those changes. The time required for the change does not matter, for it is the process of changing that changes us.

Growth is what our lives are about. Perhaps there never will be a time when things will look very much different from how they look today, but as each of us goes through our own individualized process of changing, the world is, in truth, a changed place as a result.

It is scary stuff, to change. It is unknown. It is unclear. It seems unsafe. But, in truth, if our perspectives are toward self-love, there is nothing to fear. We each have this power, inside of us, and if we can let go of our fears, that power can liberate us and others.

Exercise your power. Go with love.

Say not the struggle naught availeth,
   The labor and the wounds are vain,
The enemy faints not, nor faileth,
   And as things have been they remain.

If hopes were dupes, fears may be liars;
   It may be, in yon smoke concealed,
Your comrades chase e'en now the fliers,
   And, but for you, possess the field.

For while the tired waves, vainly breaking,
   Seem here no painful inch to gain,
Far back, through creeks and inlets making,
   Comes silent, flooding in, the main.

And not by eastern windows only,
   When daylight comes, comes in the light,
In front, the sun climbs slow, how slowly,
   But westward, look, the land is bright.[2]

NOTES

CHAPTER 1

[1]DIANE DREHER, *The Tao of Inner Peace* (New York: Harper-Perennial, 1991), p. 6 (translation of Tao 79). Copyright © 1990 by Diane Dreher. This and subsequent quotations used by permission of Donald I. Fine, Inc., original publishers.

[2]IRVIN D. YALOM, *Existential Psychology* (New York: Basic Books, 1980), p. 8. Copyright © 1980 by Yalom Family Trust. Used by permission of the author and HarperCollins.

[3]ALAN WATTS, *The Book: On the Taboo Against Knowing Who You Are* (New York: Vintage Books, 1989), p. 112. Copyright © 1966 by Alan Watts. This and subsequent quotations used by permission of the publisher.

[4]THOMAS CLEARY, trans. and ed. *The Tao of Politics* (Boston: Shambhala, 1990), p. 77. © 1990 by Thomas Cleary. Reprinted by arrangement with Shambhala Publications, Inc., 300 Massachusetts Ave., Boston MA 02115.

CHAPTER 2

[1]ALAN WATTS, *Tao: The Watercourse Way* (New York: Pantheon Books, 1975), p. 77 (paraphrased). Copyright © 1975 by Mary Jane Yates Watts, Literary Executrix of the Will of Alan W. Watts, deceased. This and subsequent quotations used by permission of the publisher.

[2]STEPHEN MITCHELL, trans., *Tao Te Ching* (New York: HarperPerennial, 1991) (tr. Tao 48). Copyright © 1988 by Stephen Mitchell. This and subsequent quotations used by permission of HarperCollins.

[3]MARILYN FERGUSON, *The Aquarian Conspiracy* (Los Angeles: Jeremy P. Tarcher, 1980), p. 85. Copyright © 1980 by Marilyn Ferguson. Used by permission of the publisher and the author.

⁴MILDRED NEWMAN and BERNARD BERKOWITZ, *How To Be Your Own Best Friend* (New York: Random House, 1971), p. 6 (emphasis added). Copyright © 1971 by Mildred Newman and Bernard Berkowitz. This and subsequent quotations used by permission of the publisher.

⁵From *All in the Family.* Used by permission of ELP Communications.

⁶NEWMAN and BERKOWITZ, *How To Be Your Own Best Friend,* p. 26.

⁷CHARLOTTE JOKO BECK, *Everyday Zen: Love and Work* (New York: Harper & Row, 1989), p. 160 (citing an old Zen saying). Copyright © 1989 by Charlotte Joko Beck. This and subsequent quotations used by permission of the author and HarperCollins.

CHAPTER 3

¹LOY CHING-YUEN, *The Book of the Heart,* trans. Trevor Carolan and Bella Chen (Boston: Shambhala, 1990), p. 25. © 1988, 1990 by Trevor Carolan and Bella Chen. This and subsequent quotations reprinted by arrangement with Shambhala Publications, 300 Massachusetts Ave., Boston, MA 02115.

²WATTS, *Tao: The Watercourse Way,* p. 75 (paraphrased).

³WATTS, *Tao: The Watercourse Way,* p. 23 (tr. Tao 2).

⁴SHUNRYU SUZUKI, *Zen Mind, Beginner's Mind* (New York: Weatherhill, 1970), p. 41. This and subsequent quotations used by permission of the publisher. Protected by copyright under the terms of the International Copyright Union; all rights reserved.

⁵DREHER, *The Tao of Inner Peace,* p. 164 (tr. Tao 64).

⁶KURT VONNEGUT, *Cat's Cradle* (New York: First Laurel Edition, 1988), p. 13. Copyright © 1963 by Kurt Vonnegut. Used by permission of the publisher.

[7]WATTS, *The Book*, p. 13 (paraphrased).

[8]BECK, *Everyday Zen*, p. 126.

[9]WATTS, *The Book*, p. 31.

[10]Parallax is seeing an object from two different positions. The simple example is to close one eye and focus on a distant object, noting its position. Then open that eye and close the other, looking again at the object. It will appear to be in a slightly different position. There seems to be movement of the object even though there is none. Astronomers can fix the distance of the object by knowing the distance between the two points of observation.

[11]ERIC HOFFER, *The True Believer* (New York: Perennial, 1966), p. 67. Copyright 1951 by Eric Hoffer. Used by permission of HarperCollins.

[12]RAY GRIGG, *The Tao of Relationships* (New York: Bantam, 1989), p. 19. Copyright © 1988 by Humanics Limited, Atlanta, GA 30309. This and subsequent quotations reprinted with permission from Humanics Limited.

[13]SUZUKI, *Zen Mind, Beginner's Mind*, p. 41.

[14]BECK, *Everyday Zen*, p. 155.

[15]GRIGG, *The Tao of Relationships*, p. 25.

CHAPTER 4

[1]DREHER, *The Tao of Inner Peace*, p. 201 (tr. Tao 67).

[2]GRIGG, *The Tao of Relationships*, p. 9.

[3]GERALD JAMPOLSKY, *Love Is Letting Go of Fear* (Berkeley: Celestial Arts, 1970). Copyright © 1970 by Gerald G. Jampolsky and Jack O. Keeler. Used by permission of the author and the publisher.

[4]MARSHA SINETAR, *Do What You Love, The Money Will Follow* (New York: Dell, 1989), p. 24 (paraphrased). Copyright © 1987 by Dr. Marsha Sinetar. Used by permission of the publisher.

[5]BECK, *Everyday Zen*, p. 72.

[6]NEWMAN and BERKOWITZ, *How To Be Your Own Best Friend*, p. 16.

[7]HERB GOLDBERG, *The Hazards of Being Male* (New York: Signet Books, 1976), p. 46 (paraphrased). Copyright © 1976 by Herb Goldberg. This quotation and next used by permission of the author.

[8]GOLDBERG, *The Hazards of Being Male*, p. 15.

[9]GRIGG, *The Tao of Relationships*, facing page.

CHAPTER 5

[1]MITCHELL, trans., *Tao Te Ching* (tr. Tao 4).

[2]HENRY DAVID THOREAU, *Walden* (New York: Holt, Rinehart and Winston, 1961 [1854]), p. 181.

CHAPTER 6

[1]CHING-YUEN, *The Book of the Heart*, p. 52.

[2]ARTHUR HUGH CLOUGH, "Say Not the Struggle Naught Availeth" (1849), in *Poetry of the Victorian Period*, edited by George Benjamin Woods and Jerome Hamilton Buckley. (New York: Scott, Foresman and Company, 1955), p. 410.